11-17-10

To JANET - KIDDO
AND HER GREAT
SENSE OF HUMOR !
Love Always,
Noreen - Kiddo

St. Trinian's

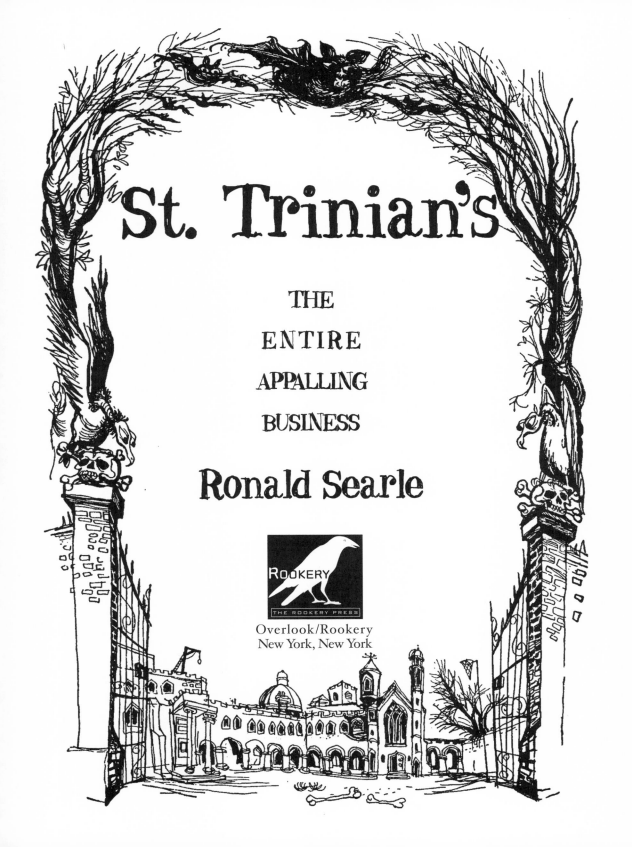

St. Trinian's

THE
ENTIRE
APPALLING
BUSINESS

Ronald Searle

Overlook/Rookery
New York, New York

ST. TRINIAN'S

This edition first published in The United States of America in 2008 by
The Rookery Press, Tracy Carns Ltd
in association with The Overlook Press
141 Wooster Street
New York, NY 10012
www.therookerypress.com

Cataloging-in-Publication Data is on file at the Library of Congress

Printed in the United States of America
FIRST EDITION

ISBN 978-1-58567-958-4
ISBN-10 1-58567-958-5

1 3 5 7 9 10 8 6 4 2

Contents

INTRODUCTION   vi

THE DRAWINGS   11

1. Welcome to St Trinian's!   12

2. Sports Days   66

3. Love at St. Trinian's   80

4. St. Trinian's Abroad   98

5. 6th Form   114

6. Christmas & New Year's & Home for the Hols   136

7. Back to the Slaughterhouse   156

8. St. Trinian's: The End   162

INTRODUCTION

PUBLISHER'S NOTE:

In a post-Hogwarts world, English boarding school life needs little introduction. The camaraderie and the sporting contests, the headmasters and mistresses, school uniforms and first love, and above all, the eye-opening intimation that life has a dark side and childhood innocence an end—all form a world apart under the dizzying spires and gargoyled walls of an ancient Gothic institution. But before Hogwarts, there was another fictional English boarding school . . . It was called St. Trinian's School for Girls, and its name called up all that is unruly and unholy and high-spirited and utterly terror-inducing to conformist society. But, to which add, clever and resourceful and engaging and charming and ever so brave. The schoolgirls of St. Trinian's, created—drawing by mordantly funny drawing—by the elegantly twisted pen of Ronald Searle, represent a world as dark and bewitching in its way as that now very famous school for witches and wizards.

The first Ronald Searle schoolgirl cartoon appeared in 1941, the second in 1946, and the remainder between 1947 and 1952. Kaye Webb, who was to become the legendary publisher of Puffin books, was, at *Lilliput* magazine, the first publisher (and later the first wife), of Ronald Searle.

It is a pity I cannot remember their actual arrival, but we clearly thought them promising, for also in the file recording his early efforts is a letter, signed by me, saying that *Lilliput* would buy three of R. Searle's cartoons, including "the one about the schoolgirls." He promptly sent off another batch, but before he learned their fate, or had the pleasure of seeing the others in print, the ill-fated 18th Division, of which Searle's company was part, had embarked for "an unknown destination."

So in February 1942, just about the time that we at *Lilliput* were wondering why the promising young Ronald Searle had not submitted any more cartoons, the artist, more or less in the middle of a battle, was stooping to pick up an abandoned copy of the October issue from the pavement of a Singapore side street. Two minutes later, sheltering from Japanese mortar bombardment, he found himself gazing at the first St. Trinian's drawing to be published. The caption, slightly reworded, said:

"Owing to the international situation,
the match with St. Trinian's has been postponed."

In the same issue, a few pages further back, there appeared a photograph of a satisfied-looking group of Japanese soldiers and opposite it a clutch of cowering monkeys.

Twenty-four hours later, with the magazine carefully rearranged to separate these two photographs, and stowed into his map pocket, Searle and his companions had obeyed the order to surrender and were being marched off on the first stage of their painful journey to the prison camp in Changi.

Owing to the international situation, the career of cartoonist Ronald Searle had been postponed. This improbable story is entirely true.

And this, of course, is the explanation of the four-year gap between the appearance of the first and second schoolgirl cartoons, and to those students of humor who are observant enough to notice it, the difference in mood between that first gentle little gibe at the circumscribed world of young females and the others which followed immediately afterwards.

The first, as we have established, was drawn more or less unintentionally, without any particular aim in mind. But when life in the unspeakable squalor of the Japanese prison camp had assumed some sort of pattern, Searle, squatting in the corner of a hut with his cunningly-preserved fountain pen, and paper stolen from the Japanese, started drawing again. And he drew for the future, for the career he would take up again when they all got out. For the edification of those at home he recorded the conditions of his companions, for his own pleasure and relief he drew . . . funny pictures.

A joke about schoolgirls had been successful; so, naturally, he tried working on another one. But it was inevitable that the debacle he had just witnessed, the atmosphere of cruelty and the smell of death in which he and his companions existed for the next four years, should permeate his drawings so that the next two schoolgirl jokes took on their first flavor of violence. It hardly seems necessary to mention that Searle does not really think of schoolgirls as murderous little horrors. But unconsciously he was seeking to reduce horror into a comprehensible and somehow palatable form. The second cartoon was concerned with torture, and the third with arson (although they were not eventually published in this order).

There was an almost excessive amount of grief in the offices of *Lilliput* when the news reached us that our promising young contributor was "missing believed killed" . . . and quite unreasoned delight when soon after VJ Day I read . . . that among the survivors of Changi jail was a young artist called Searle . . .

And on his return, bearing a neat folder containing seventy-two cartoons drawn in faded ink on stained and yellowing paper, crumpled from having been buried in the jungle and hidden under disease-ridden mattresses, this same young artist was received with open arms. [from *The St. Trinian's Story*, 1959]

In addition to *Lilliput*, the cartoons appeared in *Punch*, the *Times Literary Supplement*, and *Vogue* among other publications. They also graced various collections of Searle's drawings over the years, such as *Hurrah for St Trinian's*, *The Female Approach*, and *Back to the Slaughterhouse*. In 1952, The St. Trinian's girls got literary in a novel, *The Terror of St. Trinian's*, with text by Timothy Shy; the drawings from which comprise the section "Sixth Form" herein. Then, in 1953, Ronald Searle suddenly, perversely, maddeningly, did them in, sending the school up in a glorious blaze in *Souls in Torment*.

Total annihilation? Not quite. The St. Trinian's girls burnished the silver screen in five films, starting with 1954's *The Belles of St Trinian's*. Classic status was conferred undeniably in 2000 when a selection of the drawings appeared in Penguin Classics with the publication of *The Terror of St Trinian's and Other Drawings*. And now a sixth film, produced by the legendary Ealing Studios and directed by Oliver Parker and Barnaby Thompson, threatens to inflict the charmingly terrifying girls on a whole new generation—*St. Trinian's*, starring Rupert Everett in the Alastair Sim role, as both Headmistress Fritton and her brother; Colin Firth as Education Minister Geoffrey Thwaites; Mischa Barton as J.J. French; and Russell Brand as Flash Harry.

What does this tenacious longevity tell us? That Ronald Searle's St. Trinian's drawings are truly evergreen, the girls' lively, sinister charm standing undiminished through the years. The book you hold in your hands marks the first time all the St. Trinian's cartoons appear together, in one volume. Girls, girls! Welcome back!

THE
DRAWINGS

1.

Welcome
to
St. Trinian's!

"Owing to the international situation the match with St. Trinian's has been postponed."

Ronald Searle

"Hand up the girl who burnt down the East Wing last night."

"Well, that's O.K. —now for old 'Stinks.'"

"Bang goes another pair of Knuckledusters."

"Prudence is new to St. Trinian's,
I want you to take care of her, girls."

"Oh my God, she's put water with it again."

"All right! All right! I'll join the union."

THE TENTH BIRTHDAY PARTY

"Honestly, darling, you don't look a day over nine."

23

"Come along, prefects. Playtime over."

"Girls, girls! — a little less noise, please."

"Cynthia! How many times must I tell you to take the band off BEFORE *you light up . . ."*

"... of course indoor games are an extra."

"*Hard cheese, Maisie—your horse wasn't placed.*"

"Don't be greedy, Cynthia, give your sister some."

"Little Maisie's our problem child."

ST. TRINIAN'S 10th BIRTHDAY
Welcome to our Founder

R. Searle reviews his troops

"Elspeth!—Put that back AT ONCE.*"*

35

"*Some little girl didn't hear me say 'unarmed combat.'*"

"Cleaners getting slack, Horsefall."

"Ruddy music lessons . . . !"

"Shitty Stockhausen !"

"Look, Miss, the spirit of Botany."

"Dump those, they're harmless."

"Well done, Cynthia. It WAS *Deadly Nightshade."*

46

"Eunice, dear, aren't we rather muddling our patron saints?"

"Anyone else not enjoying themselves?"

"Peewit Patrol! Where are yoooou?"

"Smashing—pass the bat's blood."

"Who's there?"

"And please rain fire and brimstone on the lot."

"And this is Rachel, our head girl."

"Now ask him to abolish homework."

59

"Go on, say it — 'I promise to leave my body to Science.'"

"It reads, 'Apply match to blue paper and stand close.'"

"Bash her again. I think she moved."

2.

Sports Days

"But I only broke her leg, Miss."

"All right, then. Six to four the field."

"Fair play, St. Trinian's—use a clean needle!"

"Ruddy sportsdays..."

3.

Love
at
St. Trinian's

"*Well, you said your love knew no bounds.*"

"Oh my God, she's in love."

"I'll just die and then you'll be sorry."

"Playing with lethal weapons, a boy of your age . . ."

"Well, actually, Miss Tonks, my Soul <u>IS</u> in torment."

89

"Life will be just a hollow mockery without you, Drusilla."

"Why can't he let down his hair, or something?"

"She's just discovered that James Mason is married."

"Errol Flynn's started something, all right—marrying a girl with glasses."

"A dozen of that one, please."

4.

St. Trinian's Abroad

MILAN

"Facchinooo! Por — ter!"

*"Scusi, is this the home of
the famoso Don Camillo?"*

"It's WINE !"

"Well, what's Lollobrigida got that I haven't got?"

"O.K. Make it a Krug rosé and a packet of nuts."

"You don't happen to have a match?"

"I didn't realize it took so long."

*[Telescopic photo, taken through the window of the
ladies' room of a well-known Port Said hostelry.]*

"Could you tell me the time, please?"

5.

Sixth Form

"You devil in human shape!"

"I fear Cambridge will present you with many new and difficult problems."

Averse to Eros and cold as the Castalian spring

Angela Menace, with the battle-light in her eyes

She twisted her arm with skillful vigor

One of Angela's most frequently recurring daydreams

"My king !" she added softly.

"I can only conjecture that the crack about Dresden china referred to you."

"What's wrong with ME, *for Heaven's sake ?"*

"You fascinating swine."

"I got an idea, boy, that maybe Globular can use you."

Slow-footed Nemesis had caught up with Mr. Weisenheim

128

Her plans for the future were taking shape already

Brought down two fighting Governors with a flying tackle

Old Girls' Dinner

The intrepid girl began her downward journey,
while the whole sky rocked with cheering

The roseate end of every home-girl's dream

6.

Christmas &
New Year's &
Home
for
the
Hols

"First of all we'll list the people who'll pay us to go away."

"And God bless you, my little darling."

"O.K. kids, enough for a pint all round."

"Help me turn her—she's thawing."

"Let's give 'em Jingle Bells."

"*. . . and a cosh, and some scent, and a bicycle chain.*"

"... to flog them only once a day."

"We'd better have her examined—she's resolved to be good."

"I must not smoke pot during prayers.
I must not smoke pot during . . ."

"My baby home ! What fun we'll have !"

"Do come out, Rover,"
Susan won't bite."

"But he's quite big now, mother."

"Same old stuff."

" —and of course they're such company for each other."

"It means we must make sacrifices, darling.
Help Mummy by cutting down your smoking."

7.

Back to the Slaughter-house

"I picked it up at Euston."

"*But Miss Merryweather, you* SAID *we could bring out pets back with us.*"

". . . and tell Granny I didn't mean to burn her house down."

"*Hell! My best Scotch.*"

8.

The
End

ANNOUNCEMENT

ST. TRINIAN'S has gone. Encouraged by the success of recent atomic explosions in the Pacific, the school Nuclear Fission experts threw themselves into their experiments with renewed enthusiasm and with the help (thanks to certain old girls) of some newly acquired top secret information, achieved their objective at midnight last night. The remains of the school are still smouldering. By some miracle the statue of our patron saint, scorched but uncracked, still stands where once the ripple of girlish laughter could be heard on a clear frosty morning. The fate of the teaching staff is unknown, nay, will never be known, and a few young ladies are believed to have survived. Early morning reports from various parts of the country bring news of blackened figures silently trotting through sleeping villages, but bloodhounds have failed to pick up a scent—however radioactive. This blow from which St. Trinian's cannot recover (the building fund has been embezzled anyway) may bring a sigh of relief to many a parent and a quiet tear from true lovers of healthy girlhood. Let it suffice for us to say (before we draw a veil over the last broken limb) we are proud that the name of St. Trinian's has echoed through this land.

R. S.

OBITUARY

St. Trinian's

1941 – 1953

A flood of terrifying girls poured in

Debagging Old Flannelpants

A shrieking horde of Lower School types

All was well

THE END

"If you ask me, Cyril, it is not the behavior of a sahib."

"Cynthia, you really ARE *The End."*